# THE 3 QUESTIONS EVERYONE SHOULD ANSWER THAT WOULD MAKE THE WORLD A BETTER PLACE

Bryant K. Smith

The 3 Questions Everyone Should Answer That Would Make The World A Better Place
Copyright © 2025 by Bryant K. Smith

Cover Design by Bryant K. Smith. Cover photograph by Alesia A. Smith Cover copyright © 2025 A. Black Man's Press.

The scanning, uploading, copying of this book without written permission is theft of the authors intellectual property. If you would like permission to use material from the book (other than for review purposes), please contact us at Bryant@smithcan.com. Thank you for your support of authors rights.

A. Black Man's Press is a division of Smith Consulting And Networking.

ISBN: 979-8-9945815-9-9

# DEDICATION

This book is dedicated to my brother and his friends, collectively known as "The Cold Blooded Men". These men showed me how to have fun, how to how to be a friend, and how to ask questions. I appreciate all of the lessons that you taught me by simply allowing me to hang out with you. You took me to sporting events, allowed me to dj your parties, and showed me what being in community at a PWI looked like.

I not only gained a group of older brothers who looked out for me, protected me, and helped me grow, I gained confidence to be my unapologetic and authentic self. I learned to take a game and turn it into a framework for helping others to also see and be their authentic selves. This book is my gift to the world, and my thank you note and love letter to each of you.

# TABLE OF CONTENTS

| | |
|---|---|
| Preface | 7 |
| Introduction | 11 |
| 1 The First Question | 13 |
| 2 Understanding Your Boundaries and Values | 23 |
| 3 The Second Question | 29 |
| 4 Defining Your Ultimate Sacrifices | 43 |
| 5 The Third Question | 49 |
| 6 Embracing Your Purpose | 59 |
| About The Author | 69 |
| Other Books By Bryant K. Smith | 71 |

# PREFACE

If I were to tell you that your answers to three questions could tell me everything that I need to know about you, as well as tell me everything that you hold near and dear, you would think I were either a psychic or insane. After all, what three questions could I ask that would give me such insight into who you are as a person?

When I was 14 years old I learned how to play a game that would ultimately change my life. The name of the game was, "Questions". The rules of this game were simple. Sit in a circle with a group of people. Select a person to go first. That person has to make eye contact with a single person in the circle and ask that person a question consisting of three words or more, while maintaining the eye contact. In turn, the person who was asked a question has a limited amount of time to make a decision. They could look back at the person who asked the question to them or choose another person within the circle to make eye contact with and ask them a question consisting of three words or more. The goal of the game is to continuously ask questions, looking directly at the person you are questioning while making sure to never answer questions that are posed to you. It sounds simple at first and unchallenging however, we as human beings are programmed to try and answer every question posed to us. Answering questions is human nature. The game was made more challenging by having consequences for those who mistakenly answered questions that were posed of them, or if they were not quick enough to respond with a question of their own. Most often the consequences of answering a question or being unable to form a question of your own included having to consume varying amounts of some alcoholic beverage. The longer you played the game the more mistakes you were prone to make, the more mistakes you made resulted in your having to consume more quantities of alcohol. The more quantities of alcohol you consumed the more mistakes you were bound to make, and the more questions you were bound to answer. For most participants playing this game became a vicious cycle of drinking alcohol after the first time you mistakenly answered a question.

By the time I was 18 years old and a college freshman I had become a master at playing "Questions". I had learned how to quickly craft questions that would either elicit an immediate response from other players, or embarrass them to the point of silence which would also result in their having to consume alcohol for their failure to keep the game going. I also learned how to ignore simple questions that the average person would feel compelled to answer such as, "What is your name?", and how to disregard more stimulating questions such as, ",Would you like to sleep with me tonight?". I played the game of 'Questions" for so long that my mind became immune to being questioned. I became so adept at ignoring questions that I thought of it as a new skill and spent endless hours trying to master this skill.

My belief in my new skill gave me a false sense of security and power over my peers. I reasoned, erroneously, I might add, that my ability to ignore questions and to ask questions better than my peers meant that I was better, smarter, wittier and overall more intelligent than they were. In my mind, being able to ignore questions made me more mentally focused than my peers. In hindsight, I see that I was not more mentally focused than they were, just more mentally disciplined. I practiced ignoring questions and making up new questions as much as my student athlete roommates practiced their individual sports. I always looked for more opportunities to ignore people and their questions, or ways to shock and embarrass people with questions of my own. I was extremely fond of taking advertising slogans and combining them with lewd questions causing even the most seasoned "Question" players to blush, pause and have to take a drink. One of my favorite questions involved a certain soft drink beverage and my quizzing other players aloud, "If I were to place a can of said beverage in your butt would you catch the wave?" An obvious play on the beverages popular ad campaign.

I played the game "Questions" consistently from the time I was 14 years old until I was 25 or 26 years old, all the time not knowing or even conceiving that my love of questions would one day help me help so many others. I find it quite ironic that my interest in questions which I once used, or more accurately abused, in order to be amused by people is now the very same vehicle for my helping people. I'm not sure that I understood the true value asking questions had in bringing about change until I started my own work mentoring college students. It was something about sitting across the table posing what I thought were simple questions to those young people that sparked an awakening in me unlike any other I have ever experienced. I watched in confusion and disbelief as young people struggled with questions and concepts that I had taken for granted over the years. Questions like, "What do you want to do after you get out of school?", or "Who's your role model?" The students in my workshops had the same looks of bewilderment on their faces as the people I had played the game of "Questions" with over the years, only now the stakes were much higher. Making a mistake or being unable to answer the questions did not mean you were going to have to take a drink, it meant you might not graduate. It meant you might not have ever been exposed to a person you thought worthy of being a role model. It meant that no one else had ever invested the type of time needed to truly help this person to see beyond the present and plan for their future.

As my work expanded to conducting trainings for athletic teams, corporations and community agencies I discovered that many adults were not prepared to answer most basic questions either. As a communications instructor I know and understand the value of being able to articulate your thoughts verbally and I understand the importance of critical thinking, listening, and the need to be clear and concise in most conversations. Albert Einstein once said, "If you can't explain it simply, you don't understand it well enough." I agree with Professor Einstein, most people don't understand themselves well enough to answer questions that communicate their values, hopes, dreams and fears. This inability to identify and discuss what you care about or who you care about can have long term consequences on your happiness.

# INTRODUCTION

This book has been written with the reader in mind. The goal of the book is to help the reader identify what is most important and sacred to them. The questions are simple yet complex. Answering the questions requires the reader to spend some time in reflection on the experiences of their past and their desires for their future.

This book is written to expand the readers identify the values they believe in, the principles they would fight for and the causes they believe are worthy of their energies. It is a lesson in critical thinking because it forces the reader to ask more questions in order to come up with three answers to the main three questions posed by me as the author. Each chapter takes the reader on a journey into their own mind. It will require the reader to wrestle with their notions of right, wrong, ambition, sacrifice, and commitment. Odd chapters present the questions, while even chapters present the reflection activities that will assist the reader in their search for answering each of the three questions.

The final goal of the book is to help readers create consistency in their lives around the three questions. I don't propose to tell the reader what is right or wrong by posing the three questions, I simply want to help them be more intentional in how they live their lives. I firmly believe that living with intention is the best way to make the world a better place. So many people spend their lives living through happenstance and without intention that the world is deprived of their brilliance. This book hopes to give everyone a chance to shine and make the world a better place.

# 1. THE FIRST QUESTION

The first time I used this question I was shocked by the responses I received. I was working with a group of youth in a community center in Decatur, Illinois. I had written a grant for a program I created called, "Life Station". It was a male development seminar designed to help boys transition into men. The teenagers in my workshop were all African-American and ranged in age from 14 through 17. Socio-economically they would all qualify for free and reduced lunch. Some came from single parent homes, one or two had never met their fathers. In short this was a group of young males that needed some guidance and assistance in planning their futures because according to the researchers, statistics and haters, their futures didn't look too bright. Life Station was my way of trying to do my part to help them to be able to help themselves.

We sat on the floor in a large circle with each boy being given paper and something to write with I scribbled the question on the flip chart in the middle of the group and read the question aloud asking them to write their answers down.

"What would you kill a person over?", I said.

I expected silence as I gave them two answers they could not use. "You can't say your family, and you can't say your God, religion or the supreme being you believe in." My reasoning for excluding those two thing was simple. We all love our mothers, if someone were to attack them I believe even the most reasonable among us would resort to any means necessary including violence and murder to save or avenge her. Second, if you truly are committed to your religion and believe in a supreme being, regardless of what that faith system is, if that supreme being which you believe in appeared before you and told you to kill someone, I believe you would do it. Everything else was fair game to use when answering this question.

Almost immediately the young males began answering aloud. They had no problem identifying material things that they were willing to kill a person over. "Mess with my Jordan's you dead, Mr. Smith", proclaimed one boy.

"Money, if I need it and I know you got it and you won't give it to me, I'd kill you for it.", replied another from the opposite side of the circle. There was no shortage of answers and comments from the group. Only one boy stated, "I don't know, not sure I would kill anyone." He said it in a soft-spoken voice with an almost apologetic tone. At first I wasn't sure that the other boys had heard his statement. However, in unison, they almost immediately responded to his answer by calling him, "crazy, weak, and a fool". One boy who I think was the oldest in the group loudly exclaimed, "Man if you ain't ready to kill someone then you might as well be ready to die, these streets ain't nice."

I have never forgotten those words nor the look of seriousness on his face as he uttered them. I thought to myself how could you be 17 and have developed this mentality? I had them continue the exercise by writing the things they would be willing kill for on their paper. Once they had completed writing their list I asked them to share what they had written on their papers. Their list were long and varied. It included everything from money to girlfriends to cars and gym shoes. However, there was one item on everyone's list that was the same, "Respect". They had all written respect, even the boy who had said he didn't think he could kill someone asked if he could write respect after hearing the first boy read it from his paper. As we discussed their answers it became clear that none of them could clearly articulate what they meant by respect but they all knew when they felt they had been disrespected, and they all believed it was an offense worth killing another human being over. We spent so much time on that discussion that we ended our session that day before I had a chance to ask the other two questions.

From that day forward I understood I had stumbled onto something with this one question that would change the way I thought about the power of the question. It would become a hallmark in my work with youth. Eventually I would add it to the work that I did with other groups as well. This simple question deserves a more thorough examination.

What would you kill a person over, your family and your religion (supreme being) are a given? On the surface it seems that the obvious answer would be, "I wouldn't kill another human being." However, after traveling the United States of America asking thousands of people this question I know that the majority of people in the United States of America has at least one thing they would be willing to kill a person over. It doesn't matter their race, gender, sexual orientation, socio-economic status, religious belief, or even their age. The vast majority of people I have posed this question to always have at least one answer to this question.

I am not as concerned that they have found something that they believe would justify their killing another human being. I am concerned however, that the majority of things they are willing to kill over are materialistic. It is almost as if when I ask

"What are you willing to kill a person over?", they hear "What material thing are you willing to kill a person over?" Adding one word makes the question very different from what I was inquiring. Right away people attempt to answer this question by listing items that have material worth and value as opposed to listing concepts or personal values that they are willing to kill over. Somehow they rationalize that killing over items which have a universally understood value to them is better than killing over an idea or concept which they cannot see or hold. The one exception to that rule of course was they all were willing to kill over the concept of respect. In their mind killing another person over a material good was justified because they had worked hard to purchase the material item which made it theirs without question. Anyone who would try and take their material goods but was not willing to work and save as they had done in order to purchase the material item was not worthy of living and should be killed by them. In reaching this conclusion they were actually saying that the material item they had worked hard to purchase had more value than the life of a person who would attempt to take the material item from them. A jacket was worth more than a human, a pair of gym shoes was worth more than a human, a gold chain, a watch, a car, a bicycle all were worth more than a human being.

The more we discussed what they were wiling to kill another person over the more the conversation led into how they would kill another person. I was not surprised that the majority of the young men in that first group were willing to kill people with guns. The United States of America is a nation of people who believe in the ownership and use of firearms. We value our constitutional right to bear arms unlike any other people in any other part of the industrialized world. We grow up watching countless acts of violence perpetrated on television and in films, shown on the evening news and glorified in history lessons throughout our formal education. In some regard you might say that accepting killing someone with a gun is as American as apple pie. We are desensitized by the very notion that shooting someone is inhumane. Death by gun is somehow more honorable than other forms of murder. We romanticize gun violence to an extent that enables us to believe that a gun is as essential of a tool to the average citizen as a screwdriver is. Everyone may not have a gun, but everyone sure does need at least one gun is how we are raised to think about guns in the United States of America. After all you don't want to be the person who unfortunately ends up bringing a knife to a gunfight, or worse showing up to one empty handed.

There are other points that this question should make us pause and reflect on. After conducting workshops and asking more than several thousand people the question, "What would you kill a person over?" I have learned a lot more about people based on what they did not mention when answering this question. No one has ever said I would kill a person in order to get a job or a promotion. No one has ever said I would kill a person in order to join a fraternity or sorority. I have never heard anyone say that they would gladly and easily kill another person in order to avoid some sort of punishment, yet everyday people make those decisions which in some cases result in someone's death. Far too often we say or do things with little regard to the consequences of what we say or do. No one ever says I will kill someone because of their social media post yet we have lots of unfortunate examples where people have decided that what someone said about them on social media was reason enough for them to take a life, sometimes enough to even take their own life.

In the corporate world I have trained hundreds of managers and executives and none of them have ever said they would kill someone over an evaluation. However, with the stroke of a pen or the tone of their voice they may have just indirectly killed another person.

Kimberly was an African-American executive at a company whose headquarters was in suburban Charlotte, NC. She had held her mid-level executive position with her company for 21 years and was well respected in the company and in their industry. One day her Supervisor, who was a Vice President retired unexpectedly leaving a vacancy in the position. Kimberly having worked at the company thought this was a perfect opportunity for her to be promoted and become a Vice President. She submitted her application and was granted an interview. At the same time a Senior Vice President at the company, for whatever reason, had decided to make sure that Kimberly would not be promoted. She did everything in her power legal and illegal to sabotage Kimberly's application and have her removed from the candidate pool. Subsequently Kimberly did not receive the promotion, and was never quite the same in her position. A year later Kimberly left the company and became a Vice President at another competing company.

Now on the surface it looks as if everything worked out for Kimberly, but lets take a look at Kimberly's situation through a different and more comprehensive lens. Kimberly having lived in that same community for more than 21 years had become entrenched in that community. She had raised her own three children in that community, and was now living ten minutes away from her grandchildren. Her parents were still living in Detroit in the same area they had raised Kimberly and her siblings in. Unfortunately, her father had become ill around the same time that Kimberly was applying for the position that her supervisor had left vacant. One of the reasons Kimberly wanted the promotion so badly was because the increase in her salary would allow her to build her forever home and move her aging parents into the "in-law" suite that she had dreamed of. Her father's doctor had thought the move to a different climate might be good for his health and help to prolong his life. Kimberly definitely thought having her parents closer would enhance their quality of life as life in suburban Charlotte, NC was calm and quiet in comparison to the harsh realities of life in inner city Detroit, Michigan. When Kimberly did not get the promotion that she was more than qualified for, she could not ask her parents to move to Charlotte since she was no longer certain if, or for how much longer she would be living there and working for that company.

Kimberly was aware of how her candidacy had been deliberately sabotaged by the Senior Vice President and had filed the appropriate complaints through the companies human resources office. The process was long and exhausting. Eventually it was revealed that the Senior Vice President had promised the position to a friend of hers, and that she also held a bias against Kimberly because she did not want a Black woman to be a Vice President at the company. Kimberly would have been the first Black female Vice President and the only female, Black Vice President in the company. Even with those revelations her complaint was still unsuccessful in providing Kimberly with the type of relief she expected. She had hoped to be placed back in the candidate pool and allowed to compete for the position fairly and unencumbered. A less qualified Black male with less experience than Kimberly, was eventually hired as her supervisor and given the Vice Presidents job that she had applied for. She was now labeled as disgruntled by the same Senior Vice President who had sabotaged her advancement and her reputation within the company was negatively impacted. Although everyone in her department knew what had happened to her, and had seen how the Senior Vice President had intervened in the hiring process and manipulated the hiring process, no one spoke up for her.

This experience changed how Kimberly viewed her employment with the company and made her feel devalued as a person and employee. She knew she would have to leave the company and possibly the community that she had come to love. Kimberly had given a lot to the community. She was very active in the community having served as a volunteer basketball coach for at least 16 of her 21 years living in the community. Her coaching helped countless numbers of her former players to attend and graduate from college. She was active in her church, singing in the choir, serving on the usher board, and several women auxiliaries. She was a former PTA President at the local middle school and a known figure in the local political scene, now she would possibly have to walk away from all of those things and start again in a new location.

Three months into the complaint process Kimberly was offered a different position in the company as a means of resolving her complaint against the Senior Vice President. The new position was not the equivalent of the Vice President position that she would have had, and it did not have the same salary range either but it was a slight promotion, and allowed her to not have to be in the same unit with the Senior Vice President she had filed a compliant against. She accepted the position however, the company never fully staffed her new unit as they had promised and Kimberly was once again disappointed in how she was being treated. To add to her worries her father had now taken a turn for the worse and was now in the hospital in the intensive care unit. His physical decline had been brought about in part by the poor air quality and harsh winter weather in Detroit. It seemed as if nothing was going well for Kimberly. Another four months passed and Kimberly was dealt a final devastating blow when her father after a long hospital battle passed away. He had died peacefully in his sleep, but Kimberly in essence, had been mentally killed even though she was still physically alive.

"What would you kill a person over?"

Whenever I think about Kimberly and her story I am reminded of how different the outcome might have been if at some point the Senior Vice President who sabotaged her advancement would have been given some training that would have required her to think about, answer and process the question, "What would you be willing to kill a person over?". In some ways, I would argue that her attitude and subsequently her behavior, deliberately sabotaging Kimberly's career advancement had actually killed two people. One being Kimberly's father, the other being Kimberly herself. Now you may be thinking, "Wait a minute Bryant, thats one heck of a leap you are making buddy", but is it? Had she not interfered in the search process by all accounts according to the human resource report that was completed after Kimberly filed her complaint and it was investigated, Kimberly would have been selected as Vice President. She would have then felt secure that she had found the company that she would retire from and the community she would live in for the next decade or two before retiring. She would have then moved her parents to Charlotte and her father would not have spent another harsh winter in Detroit battling an illness that could have been helped, if not cured by him being in a different climate. I did not say that she planned on killing anyone, I simply stated that by her attitude and actions she was in part responsible, and therefore by default had answered the question that she was willing to kill another person over a job, a promotion, an opportunity.

You may also be saying to yourself, "Bryant, Kimberly is still alive, so how can the Senior Vice President have killed her, she's still alive? Most religions teach that within every human there are three beings that live, the mental self, the spiritual self, and the physical self. This belief is generally mirrored in Christianity in the holy trinity of the father, the son, and the holy spirit. Physically Kimberly was still alive, however it is spiritually and mentally that she had been killed. I suggest that the Senior Vice President killed her spirit and her mentality when she arranged for Kimberly to be removed from the search process by being deliberately deceitful and manipulating the hiring process. In many ways killing someones spirit and their mentality is far worse than killing them physically. When you kill someone physically there is a justice system that can at least prosecute you and charge you with murder. The people who mourn your loss can have some chance at being made whole by watching the accused go through a trial with the possibility of their being convicted.

Those same people who have to witness their friends, loved ones, and colleagues go through a spiritual and mental death have little to no recourse in which to turn in order for them to find comfort. Kimberly, if she had been physically killed would have been mourned, and would not be reliving the mental and spiritual death everyday as she interacts with colleagues, reports to a new, lesser qualified, supervisor while simultaneously mourning her fathers passing. Kimberly would not be continuously stressed with the daunting task of having to relocate after living for so many years in the same community, not because she wanted to relocate but because she could not accept the manner in which she had been treated.

# 2. UNDERSTANDING YOUR BOUNDARIES AND VALUES

## Question 1: What Are You Willing to Kill a Person Over (You cannot say your family, your God, nor your religion)?

## Introduction

This question may seem extreme at first, but it forces you to examine the limits of your moral and ethical boundaries. It challenges you to consider what principles, values, or injustices are so significant to you that they would compel you to take the most drastic action possible. By exploring this question thoughtfully, you gain a deeper understanding of what truly matters to you and how those values shape your decisions and interactions with the world.

## Activity 1: Defining Your Core Values

Before answering the question, take a moment to reflect on what you believe in. Use the list below as a starting point and circle the five values that resonate with you most.

| | | |
|---|---|---|
| Justice | Human Rights | Courage |
| Freedom | Loyalty | Equality |
| Honor | Respect | Truth |
| Integrity | Fairness | Love |

Using your five selections, rank them in order of importance.

1)_____

2)_____

3)_____

4)_____

5)_____

**How do these values influence your daily life and decision-making?**_____

_____

## Activity 2: The Moral Dilemma Reflection

Consider the following scenarios. Write down your thoughts on whether you believe taking another person's life would ever be justified in these situations. Why or why not?

**1) You witness a person attempting to kill an innocent stranger. You have a weapon and the ability to stop them. Would you act knowing it would cause that persons death?**
**My Response:**_____

_____

**My Justification:**_____

_____

THE 3 QUESTIONS...

2) A corrupt leader is oppressing people and committing violent acts against innocent individuals. You are given the opportunity to eliminate this person. Do you take action knowing eliminating them means you would cause that persons death?

My Response:_____

_____

_____

My Justification:_____

_____

_____

3) Someone is threatening your way of life—perhaps through laws, control, or force. At what point do you believe violence that may result in someones death becomes a justified response?

My Response:_____

_____

_____

My Justification:_____

_____

_____

## Activity 3: Exploring Your Ethical Line

Now, return to the original question. Write your response in a single sentence:

1) What are you willing to kill a person over (excluding family, God, and religion)?
*I would be willing to kill a person if...*_____

_____

_____

Ask yourself the following questions:

1) Does this answer align with the core values that I selected?_____

_____

_____

2) Is my answer rooted in emotion, or logic?_____

_____

3) If everyone shared my belief, would the world be a better or worse place?_____

_____

_____

## Final Reflection: Transforming Beliefs into Action

While this question forces us to think about extreme situations, its true purpose is to help us define what we stand for —and, just as importantly, what we can do to uphold those beliefs without resorting to violence.

Write down three actions you can take to protect and promote your most important values in a peaceful, constructive way:

1) _____

_____

2) _____

_____

3) _____

_____

By understanding the lines we would never cross and the values we refuse to compromise, we become more intentional about the way we engage with the world. The goal isn't just to know what we would fight for—but to actively build a world where such choices never have to be made.

# 3 THE SECOND QUESTION

On the second day of the male development seminar we reviewed the first question and the young males answers to it. They were eager to see what the second question would be. Since I had their attention I waisted no time. We moved to our reflection circle and prepared to engage. I placed the flip chart in the center and asked the young men to pull out their notebooks, then I wrote the following on the flip chart. "What are you willing to die for?" There was a deep silence in the room. I interrupted that silence by offering the same caveats that I had offered for the first question. You are not allowed to say that you are willing to die for your family, or your God, religion or supreme being.

There was still a great deal of silence in the room. The young males looked around the room as if they were searching for an answer outside of the circle. Occasionally they looked up at one another to see if anyone was writing. I looked out at them and repeated the question and the instructions. I asked them if they understood the question, and they all nodded their heads stating their understanding of the question. One young man stated, "I understand Mr. Smith but I don't like the question". His comments generated another round of head nods from his cohort. It seemed they all were not as eager to share their thoughts on this question as they were on the previous days question. Their hesitancy was a good opening for me. I began by asking, "What was so different about this question?" Almost in unison three of the young males said aloud, "I don't want to die."

There are times in my life where moments play over in my head like scenes from iconic films I have watched. Hearing three young Black males say aloud, "I don't want to die." Is one of those moments. I see their young faces. I see the innocence in them. I see the fear in them. I even see a sense of angst in their eyes as they are forced to admit that they know death is an eventuality but they didn't know there would be a choice in what you could and would give your life for. As I looked around the circle at their notebooks I could see that their sheets of paper were no where as full as the page they had written what they would kill a person over. Most had only listed one or two words, a few had written nothing.

I am not sure what I expected them to write. As I stared at the mostly blank pages I realized that my mind was actually just as blank as their notebooks. I didn't know what I was willing to die for either. Perhaps thats why the second question and the looks on their faces has stayed with me so much. Maybe their images are burned into my psyche because in those moments that I stared at their faces and into their notebooks I saw myself. Grown, but childlike. Innocent, but guilty. Guilty of never having given thought to what it is that I believed in so strongly that I would be willing to give my life if need be in order to have the outcome that I wanted.

It was in that moment of indecision that I was hit with an epiphany. I looked at the group of young males and asked them to retrieve the list of items they were willing to kill a person over from the previous days question. Once they confirmed that they were now looking at their own answers to the question, "What are you willing to kill a person over?" I began. I called on one of the older males in the group. He was a tall an slender kid with an athletic build. The slight outline of a mustache had already begun to sprout on his otherwise boyish face. His complexion was dark. He was 16 years old most of the others looked at him as a leader of sorts. I asked him to share his list of things he had written as reasons he would take another persons life. I strategically selected him because I knew from our previous days discussion that he had a rather lengthy list of items that he thought were worth killing another person over.

"Respect, food, my girl, money, a car, snitching, stealing from me, my Jordans, my bike, picking on me, lying on me, trying to get me in trouble". As he read each item from his paper I could see heads nodding in agreement that most if not all of what he had on his list were things they too thought were worth killing another human being over. I even saw some of the young males adding items to their own list after hearing him read them aloud. Once he had completed reading his list I polled the group to see if there were any objections to the items he had on his list. No one objected. The discussion that ensued was more about justifying why the items on his list meant so much to each of them that they could also see themselves killing someone over each of those alleged infractions.

After allowing the supportive comments to go on for about ten minutes I asked the group for permission to ask a new question. One boy blurted out, "Aww man here comes that tricky s**t again, Mr. Smith be on one". Laughter erupted and even I had to smile as I tried to regain order in the group. "No tricks, just another question to keep our discussion going." I said, trying to reassure them that my intentions were above board.

"Go ahead", stated the young male who had read his list. The group nodding in agreement.

"Are you willing to die for the same things you said you were willing to kill a person over?" I asked. One by one I began to restate the items the young man had read from his paper. "Are you willing to die for respect?" The group passed and looked at one another before the young male whose list I was repeating stated in a loud and triumphant voice, "hell yea ain't nobody punkin' me Mr. Smith, I ain't no bitch. I will die before somebody just disrespect me." On cue the room erupted in agreement. A chorus of, "Thats right", and "For real", rang out in the circle. Everyone agreed that respect was worthy of their making the ultimate sacrifice.

Because there was so much agreement around the term I wanted to see if they would have better luck defining respect today than they had the previous day so I asked them to give me an example of the type of disrespect that would make them kill a person. Right away another young male raised his hand to answer my question. "If a dude bump into me Mr. Smith and don't apologize or say excuse me, but he just turn and look at me like I am in his way. That's disrespect, and he got be dealt with."

Again I asked a clarifying question, "And by dealt with you mean you might kill him?" His response was, "Yea Mr. Smith, can't be letting no one think I am soft like that. You get that soft label and these streets ain't nothing nice. I can't be living like that." Heads nodded in agreement as I proceeded to go through the opening his statement granted me.

"Ok I understand, and since you said you can't live like that I assume that means you are willing to die because you didn't get an apology?" The young male looked at me and paused. His face had a look of bewilderment on it. He then said, "No I am not dumb Mr. Smith, I am not dying for an apology, I would be dying to show him he couldn't just disrespect me."

## THE 3 QUESTIONS...

I have had similar conversations with people all across the country, of all ages, and all genders. Each person saying and believing that they were willing to die for one thing, not fully understanding what that thing was. Each person unable to rationalize within themselves that the reason they believe they are saying they are dying may not actually be worth dying for. They begin to process how worthless their answers are, and therefore discover that if they die for that reason their life somehow becomes worthless as well. Somehow there is a disconnect between the worth that they attributed to something and the real value of it when it comes to making the ultimate sacrifice. Reasons that justify taking the life of another always seems to be easier and more abundant than the reasons you have that support your giving your own life.

John was a 28 year old decorated Marine when he enrolled in college. He had completed two combat tours of duty and fought in some of the nations deadliest battles over seas before earning a purple heart, and an honorable discharge due to his suffering from PTSD. Once enrolled on campus he struggled to find his place among the traditional age college students and longed for the camaraderie he had found in the Marine Corps. John found himself attracted to the brotherhood displayed by members of one of the fraternities on campus. After befriending several members and researching the organization he decided that he would like to become a member of the group. He had known several men in his life who were members of that organization and admired them. He saw this as an opportunity for him to connect himself with men of similar ideas and values and as a way for him to give back to his community as well.

By his second year of college John had an extremely high grade point average, was involved in several student organizations holding a leadership position in one of those groups. He had also been volunteering at a local youth community center and was working with a veterans group helping soldiers transition back into civilian life. He finally felt that he had the qualifications that would make him an excellent candidate for membership into he fraternity. He applied and he along with four other young men were made candidates for membership.

John had heard stories about pledging and had an idea of what that would be like. He figured if he could survive boot camp and two tours of duty overseas, he could handle the rigors of pledging. Despite being told that the process would not require the servitude, and physical duress that previous members had undergone in the past to gain admission to the fraternity John knew he would not just be allowed to pay some money and sign on the dotted line and be granted membership. In fact one of the reasons that he was attracted to the particular organization was because he had heard how respected they were for having endured a hard pledge program. He was looking forward to testing himself. He had similar reasons for choosing to join the Marine Corps over the other branches of service. He loved the idea that the Marines were viewed as being tougher than the other branches of service. Despite being told that there would be no hazing by university administrators, members of the fraternity, and other officials, John knew the process would involve activities that would test him physically, mentally, and emotionally. He looked forward to it.

Not long after his application was accepted John was approached by members of the organization on the campus to ask him if he wanted to be respected or if he just wanted to be a member of the organization. If he wanted to be respected he would need to prove himself by going through a more rigorous and albeit illegal process that he could not discuss with anyone.

## THE 3 QUESTIONS...

Despite being told that these types of processes were illegal and not a requirement for admission into the fraternity, John agreed to participate in the process. He wanted to be a respected brother and he didn't mind working to earn the respect of the fraternity members.

Four weeks later John was taken to a local hospital at 6am. He was unconscious and had reportedly passed out during a fraternity initiation activity. By 8am John was pronounced dead. A subsequent investigation and police report found that John had been the victim of a brutal hazing incident. The incident involved him drinking large amounts of alcohol while being forced to do exercises and run through a gauntlet of fraternity members each talking turns physically assaulting him. John had successfully run through the gauntlet three times before passing out on his fourth attempt at completing the gauntlet. The fraternity members were charged with his homicide. Five young men pleaded guilty to manslaughter and as part of their plea deal had to explain to the judge why the tragedy occurred. All five said that they did not intend to kill John, they just wanted him to earn their respect.

The story of John is a tragedy in that it demonstrates how never fully processing the first and the second question before you find yourself in an extreme situation can lead to a tragedy. None of the five young men who plead guilty to Johns murder had ever said that they would kill a person over respect. However, none of them would have described trying to gain fraternity membership as something they would kill a person over either. The disconnect between stating something and defining something is real.

John a decorated war veteran, knowingly made a choice to participate in an illegal and unauthorized initiation process to earn the respect of the members of the organization, however he would never have said he would be willing to die in order to gain membership in the organization. John had already answered questions one and two when he joined the Marine Corps. When he swore an oath to defend the country from all enemies foreign and domestic he understood that he was willing to kill for his country and if need be he was willing to die for it. He unfortunately never connected earning the respect of future brothers as an activity that may cost him his life.

I continued to examine the answers that were given with the young men. One by one we went through the reasons that they stated were worth taking a persons life and juxtaposed them against the reasons that they themselves were willing to die. One by one their answers to the first question, what would they kill a person over, did not match their answers to the second question, what were they willing to die for?

All of the young men agreed that they would kill someone over their "girlfriend", not their wife. I made sure to ask if we were talking about a girlfriend and not a wife because a wife was part of the exclusions I had listed when I asked the question originally. They all understood and agreed they would kill over the girlfriend. From their perspective she was theirs. She was property, another material object that they had won, or purchased. They had pursued her and she was now theirs to own and protect, which might necessitate their killing someone in order to maintain their ownership of her or to protect her.

None of them was willing to die for their girlfriend. They all laughed at the idea of dying over a girl. Especially a girl who was not their wife, mother, sister, or daughter. The fact that she was someone else's daughter, or sister didn't matter. They would take a life for her but they refused to give their life for her. The code of the streets just did not allow for them to consider her worthy of dying for, although she was worth killing for. The ironic thing about the second question is that I have yet to hear young females who have answered the question say that they believe any guy is worth killing or dying for.

It seems that in our society the idea of finding a reason that would justify killing someone is much easier to find than finding a reason you would be willing to die. Dr. Martin Luther King Jr. once said, "A man who has not found something he is willing to die for is not fit to live." In writing this book I am not going to go as far as to say that anyone is not fit to live because they can't answer my second question. However, I present for your consideration that a person who has not identified something that they believe in so strongly that they would be willing to sacrifice their life in order for that thing to exist is a person who has not completely lived their life.

The purpose of my asking the second question is two fold. First, I am asking because I want to know if people have given much thought to the concept of sacrifice. Sacrifice at its core is based on your belief in something. It is your commitment to a specific outcome. It is the means that you are willing to utilize in order to actualize the outcome that you say you believe in. Sacrifice demands that you are clear about your belief in and support of whatever you are trying to accomplish. I want to know if people have given serious thought to how determined one has to be in this life in order to live a life fulfilled, absent of regret, and full of satisfaction. Everyday someone dies with their hopes and dreams unrealized. They die with a list of regrets, and activities they have never tried. They have places they have never gone. They have wrongs they have never righted, relationships they never repaired, challenges they never faced, and stances they never took.

Some will have regrets because they feared what a failed attempt would look and feel like. Others will be unfulfilled because they lacked the ambition to ask and answer the difficult question i.e. what do I believe in so strongly that I would rather die trying to achieve it, produce it, experience it, fight for it than not?

The second reason that I continue to ask people, "What are you willing to die for?" is because I want to challenge people to be consistent with how they move in the world. In my work as a consultant and speaker I am often called in to help resolve issues around difference. Someone has mistreated another person based on some real or perceived difference between them and another person or group of people. Those differences have run the gambit from racial differences, to religious differences. They have included gender differences, and age gaps. They have included political disagreements, poor management of people, physical and mental assaults, and down right abuse of all types. In working to resolve these conflicts I have never once labeled the alleged perpetrators as racist, sexist, homophobic, etc. Not that I don't believe their behaviors fall into those categories, I just don't think it is the most productive way to address and correct behavior by condemning people with a label as a starting point to our seeking resolution, clarity, and change. I do however start by pointing out the inconsistencies in their actions, and attitudes. I discuss with them how the words, deeds, and methods they utilize when engaging one person or group are not the same that they utilize when engaging with another person or group. Their reasons for the inconsistency become less important than helping them to first recognize their inconsistency.

By asking people to begin with the first question, "What are you willing to kill a person over?" and then following up with the second question, "What are you willing to die for?" I can establish a baseline for what it is they say they value, which I can then use to test their consistency. You can't say that you believe in and value a material item enough to kill for it, if you have not been equally considered that your commitment to killing may also mean that you are committed to dying over that same thing.

Ben Wilson was a Chicago high school basketball standout in the early 1980's. He was not in a gang and was an excellent student. He is quoted having said the following when he was interviewed on a talk show one day. "I have a goal and I want to be successful. and that is, you know, when I get home I study, I do my work, and go to class." One day while walking down the street after leaving school, Ben was bumped into by another teen. Instead of letting the affront go and continuing to walk, Ben decided to say something to the teen who had bumped into him. The teen turned and flashed a gun. Ben who had felt disrespected at the time was not worried by the other teen displaying his handgun. He continued to press the teen for an apology for stepping on his foot and bumping into him. The other teen shot and killed Ben, leaving a mother without her son, and the world without a future professional athlete and respected citizen.

Ben's story is a tragic example about how inconsistency can create problems. Ben like most of the young males in my group had decided that respect was something he was willing to fight for. He did not however think if might have to die for it as well.

If I can get people to think about whether the things they believe are worth killing someone over are also worth dying over, perhaps I can get people to stop being so willing to kill one another and to risk their lives over things they truly don't believe in and that don't have merit or value in a civilized world.

Every day many of us by not thinking about what it is we are willing to die for actually end up being committed to the idea that any and everything is worth dying for. We erroneously believe that any slight, regardless of how minor it is is worth dying over. By not taking the time to decide what is and is not worth devoting and giving our lives to, we actually end up dedicating and possibly giving our life to and for superfluous things that have no value to ourselves or society.

No one that I have ever posed these questions to has ever stated or listed their job as something they would give their life for. Yet and still everyone of us knows someone who has literally worked themselves to death. No one ever says that they are willing to die for a promotion, or a salary increase, but they spend countless hours trying to get the attention of their supervisors. Some will stress themselves into heart attacks and strokes due to their lack of advancement or recognition in the workplace.

I have never met anyone who says that they would give their life in order to have a BMW, Cadillac, Bentley, Ferrari, you name the model vehicle. But here again we all know people who have died trying to get the funds to purchase the vehicle of their dreams, or the home of their dreams, or even to impress the love of their dreams. All of these people have one thing in common. They never stopped to ask themselves the difficult question which would have helped them put their life and value system in its proper perspective. "What am I willing to die for?" The question begs the respondent to decide what is going to be important in their life and also makes them consider why that thing is so important? By asking that question and wrestling with the answer, we are forced to decide what it is that we truly value and what is our value system is made of. Do we value relationships or connections? Do we value material items, or commitments? Do we want a life full of treasured memories or a trove of material possessions?

Most material possessions rarely outlive the legacies that the owners of those possessions leave behind. It doesn't matter if the person was a good person or an evil one. The items that they amass during their life will rarely outlive the stories that tell how the person lived and what they did to in order to build their material gain. It is the processing and consideration of your legacy that helps humans understand that not all values are positive. The dictionary definition of a value states, " A value is a person's principles or standards of behavior; one's judgment of what is important in life, or beneficial. To have a high opinion of." Values can be positive or negative. They, like the people who adopt them can be used for good or for evil. Identifying and adhering to a negative value system can and usually does produce negative outcomes. Identifying and adhering to positive values can and usually does create positive outcomes.

Intentionality is the main thing that differentiates the outcomes. You have to be actively engaged and deliberate with selecting positive values in order to benefit from choosing a life filled with positivity. It's like playing a sport. You have to be intentional about your need to choose and practice positivity. Unfortunately, negativity is the default norm for humanity. Bad values show up everywhere as part of our human nature. We like shortcuts, we want the easy and quick path to fame and fortune. Left unchecked most of us don't operate with integrity, and thus we find ourselves willing to kill and die for reasons that defy logic. Had we been trained to pause and think about the outcome in advance of finding ourselves in certain situations for circumstances we would make better choices.

The thing that separates humanity from other forms of life on Earth is our ability to reason and make choices. Insurance companies have researched human behavior and develop rates for various genders, ages, socio-economic statuses, based on their understanding that males and females process and understand consequences very differently. That is why car insurance is generally cheaper for women at the age of 21 than it is for men at 21. Men are thought to not understand consequences until after they reach 25, which is when their auto insurance rates usually decrease. By asking people what it is that they are willing to die for I am asking them to consider the consequences of their actions and inactions in advance. I am asking them to critically think about their value system while they are not under duress.

# 4 DEFINING YOUR ULTIMATE SACRIFICES

## Question 2: What Are You Willing to Die For (You cannot say your family, your God, nor your religion)?

## Introduction

This question is not just about facing death—it's about understanding what you hold so sacred, so valuable, that you would sacrifice your own life to defend it. What principles, beliefs, or causes matter so much to you that you would give everything to uphold them?

By reflecting on this question, you will uncover the deepest parts of your identity, values, and purpose. Your answer will help clarify what truly drives you and how you can live a life that aligns with these beliefs every day.

## Activity 1: What Would You Fight For?

Before determining what you would die for, start by considering what you would risk everything to protect. Below is a list of broad concepts. Circle the ones that you believe are worth making major sacrifices for:

| | | |
|---|---|---|
| Freedom | Protect Innocent | Build Community |
| Justice | Racial/cultural identity | Save Environment |
| Human rights | | Next Generation |
| Truth | Democracy | Your Country |
| Equality | Honor | Your legacy |

Choose three concepts from your list and explain why you feel so strongly about them.

1) _____

_____

2) _____

_____

3) _____

_____

What do these choices say about your priorities and values?

_____

_____

## Activity 2: The Edge of Sacrifice

Consider the following scenarios. Write down your thoughts on how you believe you would respond.

**1) You are given the opportunity to expose a powerful, corrupt system, but doing so would almost certainly cost you your life. Would you do it**

My Response:_____

_____

_____

**My Thought Process:** _____

_____

2) A violent regime is threatening to strip away the rights of an entire group of people. If standing against them would put your life at risk, would you still do it?

**My Response:** _____

_____

_____

**My Thought Process:** _____

_____

_____

3) Imagine a moment in history where people stood up for their beliefs despite knowing they could die—civil rights leaders, freedom fighters, or whistleblowers. If you were in their position, would you have the courage to act?

**My Response:** _____

_____

_____

**My Thought Process:** _____

_____

_____

Now, reflect: Do you see a pattern in what you are willing to sacrifice yourself for?
**My Reflection:**_____

_____

_____

**My Thought Pattern:**_____

_____

_____

## Activity 3: Writing Your Legacy Statement

If you were to die for something, what would you want people to remember about you?

Write a short "legacy statement" that reflects the cause or belief you would give everything for:

**1) What are you willing to die for (excluding family, God, and religion)?**
*I would be willing to die if it meant that...*_____

_____

_____

Ask yourself the following questions:

THE 3 QUESTIONS...

1) Are you currently living in a way that reflects this belief?_____

_____

_____

2) What actions can you take today to support this cause without risking your life?_____

_____

_____

3) Would you rather live for this belief than die for it? Explain your answer._____

_____

_____

## Final Reflection: Living for What Matters

Dying for something is an extreme expression of commitment—but truly living for something requires consistent action and dedication.

Write down three ways you can actively support the values you hold most dear:

1)_____

_____

2)_____

_____

3)_____

_____

True change doesn't just come from those willing to die for something, but from those who are willing to dedicate their lives to making the world better. Your answer to this question should not only define what you care so much about that you are willing to make the ultimate sacrifice in order to see it realized, more importantly it should shape how you choose to live.

# 5 THE THIRD QUESTION

When I created the exercise for the young men in the mentoring program, I originally thought we would spend one day answering all three questions. I underestimated the value of the questions and I underestimated the complexities that come with trying to answer them. We had spent two days answering the first two questions. That was a Thursday and a Friday conversation. I was glad that I had the weekend to fully reflect on the answers that were discussed during the previous two sessions as it better prepared me to ask the third and final question. As the reader of this book you are no doubt seeking some clarity in your life around what it is that you can do to make the world a better place and yourself a better person. I would encourage you not to read this third chapter until you too have taken a day or two to reflect on how you have answered the first two questions and thought through your value system. In so doing you will be better prepared to answer this third and final question.

On Monday the young males returned to campus where we had been meeting, fresh from the challenges that a weekend at home in an under-resourced community had provided them. They walked in with a look of eager anticipation and relief. For todays discussion I changed the configuration of the room we were meeting in. I set the room up more like a classroom with tables facing the front of the room and two chairs at each of the tables for the young males to be seated. Right away one of the young men remarked, "Are we having a test today Mr. Smith?"

I paused for moment before answering. I hadn't thought of todays question as a test when I decided to change the room set-up. I really wanted to make todays discussion more formal so instead of placing the tables and chairs to the side of the room and making a circle I opted for making the room look more like a classroom or a breakout room for a seminar at a conference.

"No, no test in here today." I replied. "But I will tell you that what we discuss today will prepare you for the test that you take everyday outside of this space". I was having my Jedi moment. It wasn't a mind trick that I was using on them but I did see myself as a sort of Mace Windu, Master Jedi, teaching a class full of young Jedi Padawans (students training to become Jedi knights in the Star Wars films).

As things settled down and each young male took his seat I began by asking them to look at their answers to the first two questions from last week. I asked if any of them had anything they wanted to say or ask before I give them the third and final question. One of the young males who was usually very quiet stated that he had gone back and changed his list over the weekend. He said that he removed some things from his list of reasons he would kill a person over, but he was still unable to add anything to his list of reasons he would be willing to die for. He asked was it normal for people to not be able to list reasons that they would die for?

Before I could answer, one of his peers related a similar experience that they had spent some time over the weekend looking at their list and removing a few things he would kill for but not being able to decide what he was willing to die for either.

## THE 3 QUESTIONS...

This led to almost the entire group opening up and once again expressing their desire to live, and not to die.

"This is hard Mr. Smith, I'm only 15 and I know I only got about ten more years to live, but I don't know what I am going to die for. I just know I'm probably going to die before I am 25. Its either that or I'm going to be in jail."

The words of that 15 year old had so much in them to unpack that it raised a knot in my stomach. I remembered throwing myself a celebratory birthday party when I turned 25. I remember thinking that the reason I threw my own birthday party was because I hadn't planned on living beyond 25 either. I wasn't suicidal, I had just been bombarded with messages that said a Black male from an urban environment in the United States of America's life expectancy was less than 25 years. Having made it to 25 I decided that I needed to celebrate. As I looked out into the room I could see the other boys nodding in agreement as if they had all been given the same playbook that said you are going to die before age 25 or you will be in jail.

The third question took on a new significance to me in that moment. I need to ask them the third question to get them to see what is possible for them. I also wondered if I were ready for the answers they would give. I went to the front of the meeting room and wrote on the dry erase board, "Question 3: What are you willing to live for?" And once again I said, "You can't live for your family, or your God/supreme being. I need you to think about this one a little deeper."

With that I put on some music and asked them to think and write in their journals their answer to that question. Minutes went buy as I walked around the room looking at each young face as they sat. Some staring at the board as if searching for an answer on the board. Others holding a pen in their hand while staring at the blank pages of their journal. Others nodding their head and lip syncing the lyrics of the rap song that was providing the soundtrack of the day throughout the room. There was a different type of silence in the room. A silence where words were not being spoken aloud but it was as if you could hear the many thoughts being echoed throughout the space. Every now and then you would see a pen move, and see a face stare at the other faces in the room to see if anyone else was writing.

I was born and raised in Chicago, Illinois. As a youth I had witnessed all types of violence directed toward people. When speaking to audiences I sometimes reference my upbringing by saying I come from a place where violence is usually the go to method for resolving conflicts. I understand all too well that for some people committing acts of violence, even killing is an easy decision.

Saying the wrong thing, wearing the wrong color, being in the wrong neighborhood could all get you violently attacked or killed. I have known people who decided that their turf, their bicycle, their gym shoes, their girlfriend and their reputation were all things that they were willing to die for. In short Chicago taught me that killing and dying are quite easy for most people who have never spent sufficient time and energy in deep, reflective thought about the finality of death. They have been conditioned to think that killing and dying are both noble, just and the ultimate proof that you are brave, and manly.

Perhaps its not just the place that I grew up in, but the time that I grew up in that has made me so immune to violence and death. After all, I spent at least ten of my most formative years watching Elmer Fudd shoot and kill a rabbit. I saw Popeye resolve every problem he ever faced by digesting a can of spinach and unleashing a ton of whoop ass on everyone in his vicinity. Cowboys killed Indians every Saturday, American soldiers in war movies killed everyone. I looked on in amazement hoping to one day demonstrate that I too was manly enough to solve the worlds problems by fighting and killing or be brave enough to die trying to fight and kill the problem. I practiced unleashing death with toys like G.I. Joe, and a Red Ryder BB gun. Killing and dying was not only entertaining to me, it was an appropriate, effective, means of resolving conflict.

It wasn't until I sat in a room full of other equally miseducated young men that I realized how unprepared I was to answer the question myself. I needed the music and the extra time to remember and reflect on my life and the lives of so many people I had come in contact with so that I could find an answer and in so doing find hope and redemption. I needed to course correct myself. If you are reading this book and attempting to answer these questions you may be experiencing similar thoughts about how you have arrived at this point in your life, yet be struggling with the juxtaposition of life and death. You may be looking to fully comprehend what it means to kill, die, and live.

Malik was sitting in a closet in his home. In one hand he held a letter informing him that he did not receive the job he had interviewed for. The latest in a slew of rejection letters that he had been sent. In the other hand he held a 9mm Glock handgun, trying to find the courage to end his own life.

Malik had gone to and graduated from college, he had worked hard for his employers. He had done all of the things that he was told he needed to do in order for him to excel and bee promoted. He just knew that when the leadership position within the company came open he would be selected to fill the vacancy.

He was given an interview but was passed over for the position. It turns out that the CEO of the company had a nephew who he thought should have the leadership position despite him having never gone to college nor worked at the company. That was the reason Malik started looking for opportunities with other companies.

Malik had been a finalist with several companies but in the end there was always a reason they went with another candidate. Prior to receiving the letter that he held in his hand the recruiter who had interviewed him had called to let him know that after speaking with Maliks supervisor for a reference he was not going to be able to offer him the position. The recruiter also told Malik the things that his supervisor had said about him. According to the supervisor Malik was a sub par employee. He was always late, failed to complete assignments, was in need of constant supervision and was not a team player. Malik was crushed and confused upon hearing this report as he had just received his performance review from that same supervisor and his written performance evaluation was one hashmark from "Excellent". There was no mention of tardiness, or missed assignments. No mention of him not being a team player, just praise for his leadership of his work group and team.

Now he sat in a closet rejected, depressed, and hopeless. The only way he saw to relieve his pain and free himself from the depressed state was now staring back at him in the form of a cold black polymer and metal pistol. He searched but could not find a reason to live.

The room was about the size of a small bedroom. If I had to guess I would say it was about 12 feet, by 10 feet. There was a long rectangular table in the middle of the room with chairs placed all around the table. There were enough chairs for all ten people who were in the room. There was one tiny window covered with steel bars that was placed opposite the door which led into the room. The door had small plastic placard on it that said, "Library" on it, which made sense when one was standing on the outside of the door, but was a sense of cruel irony when you opened the door and walked in to se that there were no books, and no shelves for books in the room. It reminded me of one of those old interrogation rooms you would see on an old police television show like Dragnet, or in the film Menace To Society.

When the men entered the room it became increasingly smaller. One by one they filed in, orange pants, white, A framed t-shirts, white socks and orange plastic slide style shoes on their feet. Each one holding a stack of papers in their hands or rolled up in their back pocket. The papers were copies of my newest book on manhood, "Manhood, The Missing Manual". Institution rules forbid the men from having actual bound books as they could apparently be easily converted and used as weapons. Spines of books could have similar effects of a 2 by 4 when used as a weapon. I was in a medium security state penitentiary in Illinois. I was meeting with the men who had been reading my newest book on male development.

Sitting across from men who had been convicted of various crimes in such a small and confined space with no guards in the room and only one way in or out of the room was unsettling. Having men who were physically in some of the best shape I had ever seen men in absent an athletic team locker room was also a bit unnerving. The session however was the most insightful and engaging workshop I have ever experienced. It was one of the best exchanges of thought and self reflection that I had ever participated in. I have taught in classrooms and boardrooms but in prison I found men who had come to the session prepared to engage me in a conversation about my work, not because they wanted a promotion, not because someone in human resources required them to get a new certification, but because they were truly interested in how my book might help them to improve their lives or the lives of their loved ones.

As the session was winding down I got the last of the three questions and asked, "What are you willing to live for?" The men unlike the young males in my session in Decatur when I first began asking this question were all eager to answer right away. They had all thought about what it was they were living for. I heard answers like, "Redemption", "Hope that no one else has to come to a place like this", "Resolution", and "Forgiveness". Their words resonated with my soul in such a profound way that no matter where I am in the world and am asking the three questions their answers always seem to be at the forefront of my mind. As happy as I was to hear their heartfelt answers and to see the conviction in their eyes as they discussed what it is they were living for, it was also sad. I wondered why did they have to come to prison in order to have the time and ability to think about the joy and value of life and living?

The young men in Decatur gave me their answers and I was surprised that the majority of them without discussing their answers with one another in advance had written a similar phrase.

"I don't know what I am living for".

One by one as I looked at the words written in their journals the majority of the young males had declared they couldn't think of one reason that they thought was worth living for. Those who did identify something in their journals wrote things like, "I'm living so I can get a job and get rich". Another wrote, "I am living so I can be better than the man who left me and my mom alone".

We spent the remainder of our time together that Monday talking about the importance of identifying something that you believe in enough that everyday you want wake up and keep working towards it. I tried to connect dots by telling them that one thing you are living for should be something that you should be able to use consistently to answer all three questions without it causing you to feel conflicted in your value system. But most importantly it should be something that allows you to make the third question your first question everyday.

If you start your day with the reason that you believe you are alive, you will live. You will fight to stay alive and you will not want to be the reason that someone else does not want to be alive. The value of the three questions is not in finding the time to ask yourself the three questions, it is in ones willingness and ability to work through the process of knowing oneself well enough to provide an answer to them that is reflective and consistent. The value of the question and the answer is in your ability to critically think about each one for yourself and make adjustments to your behavior when needed.

The first adjustment you should and will make is to rearrange the order of the three questions. "What am I willing to live for?" should be the first and most important question that you ask yourself each and everyday. What you are willing to live for and your purpose should and will become tangential.

They will become intertwined in such a way that you will always have the motivation you need to meet any obstacle that is placed in your path. There is a synergy of sorts that is created when you are rooted in knowing that there is something you believe in so strongly that it provides purpose and guidance to you every day. It serves as both inspiration and a reminder that you are uniquely important and positioned to do the thing that keeps you alive.

You develop laser beam focus for living, but you also become immersed in living your life to its fullest. You will not take life for granted. You will create a life dedicated to your trying to accomplish specific projects that are worthwhile with the reassurance that you are creating and leaving a lasting legacy of positive fulfillment. The satisfaction you receive from working toward a specific outcome is the ultimate sense of fulfillment and love. By living your life everyday in pursuit of a specific reason you are demonstrating that you love yourself enough to endure the difficulties that life throws your way. You serve as a beacon of hope that lights a path that others can and hopefully will follow.

# 6 EMBRACING YOUR PURPOSE

## Question 3: What Are You Willing to Live For (You cannot say your family, your God, nor your religion)?

## Consideration

While the first two questions helped you explore your boundaries and ultimate sacrifices, this question focuses on the most important one: What is so meaningful to you that it drives your everyday existence?

Choosing what to live for requires more than just identifying a cause—it demands action, purpose, and a commitment to something bigger than yourself. This section will help you explore what truly gives your life meaning and how you can intentionally live in alignment with that purpose.

## Activity 1: Finding What Captivates You?

Before defining what you are willing to live for, let's start by identifying what excites and motivates you. Below is a list of broad concepts. Circle the ones that excite and or motivate you to act:

| | | |
|---|---|---|
| Making Money | Quality of Life | Material Items |
| Having Fun | Good Health | Being Respected |
| Friendship | | |

| | | |
|---|---|---|
| Ethnic Identity | Being Useful | Problem Solving |
| Being Helpful | Teamwork | Connections |
| Creativity | Safety | Community |
| New Opportunities | Consistency | Drama |
| | Adventure | Feeling Valued |

**Choose three concepts from your list and explain why you feel so strongly about them.**

1) _____

_____

2) _____

_____

3) _____

_____

Use the following prompts to help you further understand what captivates you:

**1) The following activities make me lose all track of time because I enjoy doing them so much.** _____

_____

_____

**2) What issues do you see in the world that ignite within you a desire to commit time energy and other resources to supporting it or fighting against it?** _____

THE 3 QUESTIONS...

_____

_____

_____

3) When was the last time you felt deeply fulfilled, and what were you doing that made you feel that way?_____

_____

_____

_____

_____

4) If you knew that you only had one year left live, what would you dedicate that time to doing?_____

_____

_____

_____

_____

_____

_____

# Activity 2: Creating Your Life Mission Statement

A mission statement is a personal declaration of what you stand for and how you intend to live your life. Fill in the blanks below to create your first draft:

"I believe the world needs more_____

_____

_____

I am committed to living a life that promotes_____

_____

_____

My actions and choices will reflect_____

_____

_____

I will dedicate myself to _____

_____

_____every day."


Rewrite your mission statement in a way that feels personal and meaningful to you:

_____

_____

# THE 3 QUESTIONS...

_____

_____

_____

_____

**Reflect: Does your current lifestyle align with this statement? If not, what changes do you need to make?**

**My Current Lifestyle Choices:** _____

_____

_____

_____

_____

**Lifestyle Changes I Need To Make:** _____

_____

_____

_____

# Activity 3: The 10-Year Vision Exercise

Envision your life 10 years from now. Answer the following:

1) If you are truly living for your purpose, what does your daily life look like?

_____

_____

_____

2) What kind of impact have you made on the people around you?

_____

_____

_____

3) What achievements or contributions have given your life deep meaning?

_____

_____

_____

_____

_____

**4) What obstacles could prevent you from fully living the life you have just envisioned for yourself? How will you remove or overcome them?**

_____

_____

_____

_____

_____

_____

_____

Ask yourself: Did I imagine or envision my life 10 years into the future? Imagination is fantasy. It's what you wish for, or hope for. Envisioning differs because it is what you plan for. It is what you will work for. You won't rely on wishful thinking or luck, you will work to fulfill that which you envision.

Take a moment to write a letter to your future self as if it's 10 years from today. What do you want to remind yourself about your purpose? What advice would you give?

## Activity 4: The Daily Purpose Challenge

Living for something requires action. Over the next 7 days, challenge yourself to do something every day that aligns with your purpose.

Document your commitment to the challenge below:
**Day 1: I will:**_____

_____

**Day 2: I will:**_____

_____

_____

**Day 3: I will:**_____

_____

_____

**Day 4: I will:**_____

_____

_____

**Day 5: I will:**_____

_____

_____

**Day 6: I will:**_____

_____

_____

**Day 7: I will:**_____

_____

_____

**At the end of the week document the following:**

**How did completing each of these actions improve your mindset and help you reflect your values and your passions?**

## Final Reflection: Your Life's Work

Many people never take the time to ask themselves what they are truly living for. Now that you have, take one final moment to write a personal declaration:

"From this day forward, I commit to living my life in support of the following principles, and concepts that I believe in. They are as follows:

_____

_____

_____

I will embody this purpose through my words, my actions, and my choices, because I believe my life is meant for something greater."

***True change doesn't just come from those willing to die for something, but from those who are willing to dedicate their lives to making the world better. Your answer to this question should not only define what you care so much about that you are willing to make the ultimate sacrifice in order to see it realized, more importantly it should shape how you choose to live.

Bryant K. Smith

THE 3 QUESTIONS...
# ABOUT THE AUTHOR

Bryant K. Smith —Bryant K. Smith is the founder, President and CEO of Smith Consulting And Networking (Smith C.A.N.), a comprehensive consulting, speaking and coaching firm. Bryant is an expert communicator who specializes in making sure that the message you want sent is the message that your audience, team, staff and students receive. Whether it is empowering your audience to value difference, practice equity, embrace change, increase productivity or live their best lives by tapping into their unlimited potential, Bryant's engaging keynotes, virtual or in-person trainings, one-on-one consultations and coaching get his audience to critically think about complex issues, find their purpose and make a difference in the world. When how it's said is just as important as what is said, you want Bryant K. Smith to say it.

Helping individuals, businesses, and educational institutions understand the importance of making sure that they invest in people has been the hallmark of Bryants professional career. For more than two decades, he has consistently been able to provide clients with immediately actionable steps and strategies that create cohesion, reduce conflicts, and enhance individuals abilities to be high achieving global citizens. He is an expert at helping males process and embrace change, redefine manhood, and work through issues which may impact their ability to be physically, spiritually, mentally and emotionally well..

A seasoned higher education administrator, competent classroom instructor and championship basketball coach, Bryant founded SmithC.A.N. in 2000 as a vehicle to better help businesses, teams and schools invest in their most valuable assets - their people. Bryant has presented to more than 1,000 audiences across the United States and in Spain as the guest of the Spanish Consulate. He has been a Director of Multicultural Affairs and International Student Services at two universities in the United States and has taught collegiate level courses in Communication, Leadership, and Popular Culture.

Bryant has created thought-provoking and award winning experiential learning programs that have helped thousands of people reframe their views on difference, communication and male development. He is the author of 10 published books and a recurring presenter and facilitator at several annual conferences on education, leadership, life skills, and personal development. Considered by many to be a thought leader on the intersections of communication and personal development, Bryant is a highly sought after speaker and facilitator. A proud product of the Chicago Public school system and beneficiary of Trio program support throughout college, he understands that hard work will always overcome hard times.

Using his uniquely engaging and thought provoking style, he both challenges and excites his audience with his critical analysis and passionate delivery. "Insightful", "Engaging", "Deep", and "Real" are all words his audiences use to describe their experiences with him. He is Bryant K. Smith, "The Human Potential Specialist".

THE 3 QUESTIONS...
# Other Books By Bryant K. Smith

www.ingramcontent.com/pod-product-compliance
Lightning Source LLC
Chambersburg PA
CBHW070551090426
42735CB00013B/3146